Basic Skills Series

INFERENCING
Using context clues to infer meaning

by
Karen Clemens Warrick

Cover Art
by
Sherry Neidgh

Cover Design
by
Peggy Jackson

Inside Illustrations
by
Linda Hohag

Publisher
Instructional Fair • TS Denison
Grand Rapids, Michigan 49544

About the Author

Karen Clemens Warrick holds a bachelor of science degree from Ball State University, as well as a master's degree in elementary education from Arizona State University. After 15 years of teaching, Karen became an author of both educational materials and biographies for children. She is a member of the Society of Children's Book Writers and Illustrators and has conducted writing workshops for teachers for the past five years. Karen lives with her husband Jim in Prescott, Arizona.

Credits

Author: Karen Clemens Warrick
Cover Art: Sherry Neidgh
Cover Design: Peggy Jackson
Inside Illustrations: Linda Hohag
Project Director/Editor: Sharon Kirkwood
Editors: Kathryn Wheeler, Wendy Roh Jenks
Page Design: Pat Geasler

Standard Book Number: 1–56822–924–0
Inferencing—Grades 1–2
Copyright © 2000 by Ideal • Instructional Fair Group
a Tribune Education Company
3195 Wilson Drive, NW
Grand Rapids, Michigan 49544

About the Book

The activities in *Inferencing* are designed to improve students' reading comprehension. The skill of inferencing, using information to draw logical conclusions, is a higher-level thinking skill—a difficult one for young students to master. Early readers need to practice the application of this skill over and over again in a variety of ways.

Inferencing requires the reader to make educated guesses based on prior knowledge and on information that is implied, but not directly stated. The high-interest lessons in this book are supplemented with a variety of activities to make learning the skill of inferencing fun. The exercises increase in difficulty as the book progresses, so the students practice more advanced skills as they work through the book.

With a variety of fun and instructional formats, teachers can provide direct instruction, reinforcement, or independent practice throughout the year. Have students work with partners or teams to complete the more challenging activities. Place the activity sheets in a center and reproduce the answer key for self-checking.

Table of Contents

Summer Fun

Look at the objects below. ✂ and 🖊GLUE pictures of those things you would find at the beach in the big beach picture above.

Try this: Draw something you'd like to see at the beach in the empty box. Cut and paste it in the picture, too.

What's Wrong with This Picture?

Look at the picture. ✎ the things that don't belong.

Try this: Draw a picture of your school room. Put four things in the picture that don't belong at school.

Ready for School

the tools you use at school.

Draw a line to the student who needs that tool.

Try this: On another sheet of paper, draw a picture of where you would use the tools not circled on this page.

In the City

✂ and 🧴 GLUE the pictures where they belong in the picture above.

Try this: Draw something you'd like to see in the city in the empty box. Cut and paste it in the picture, too.

In the Country

✎ the things that don't belong in the picture.

✏ the farm animal families below.

At the Airport

What would you find at the airport?

✂ and ![GLUE] those pictures that belong in the airport scene above.

TICKETS

Try this: Draw something you'd like to see at the airport in the empty boxes. Cut and paste them in the picture, too.

Toy Swap

Draw a line from each child to the toy he or she would like.

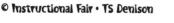 Name _____

What's Happening?

Look at the pictures in each row. ✎ the picture on the right that shows what happens next.

✎ the picture above that gave you clues about what the boy was making.

✎ the picture that gave you clues about what animal was being fed.

✎ the picture that gave you clues about what plant would grow.

Name _____

What Comes Next?

Look at the pictures. Draw a picture that shows what happens next.

What Rhymes?

Read each list of words. Then read the sentence.  the rhyming word that belongs in the sentence.

1. bed
   red
   fed
   led

   The apple on the tree is <u>bed</u>.

2. bat
   cat
   fat
   sat

   The boy's baseball <u>cat</u> is under his chair.

3. fig
   big
   dig
   pig

   The big <u>dig</u> in the barn has six pink babies.

4. boat
   coat
   float
   goat

   I put on my new <u>boat</u>.

5. brown
   down
   clown
   town

   The funny <u>town</u> had a big red nose.

6. lap
   map
   cap
   nap

   The baby needs to take a <u>map</u>.

Try this: On another sheet of paper, write as many words as you can that rhyme with the word *pan*.

Where Am I?

Read each story. Answer the questions.

1. Stacie rode the merry-go-round. She bought a ticket for a ride on the ferris wheel. Then she rode the roller coaster.
   Where is Stacie? _____

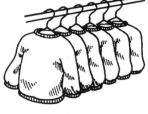

2. Paul saw the polar bears and the lion. He watched the monkeys and the gorilla. Then he walked slowly through the reptile house.
   Where is Paul? _____

3. Tina walked in the door and hung up her coat. She sat down at her desk, got out her book and began to read. She read until she was told to put her book away. Then she got ready for her spelling test.
   Where is Tina? _____

4. Karen ran to the barn to see the cows, sheep, chickens, and pony. She was always glad to visit Grandma and Grandpa. She loved to run in the fields, gather the eggs, and ride on the tractor.
   Where do Karen's grandparents live? _____

5. Tony followed Mom through the big door. First he saw men's shirts and shoes. They walked past the pants and socks. Then Tony saw racks of dresses. They went to the second floor and found clothes for kids.
   Where are Tony and his mom? _____

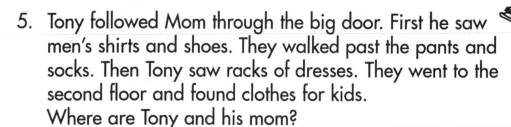

Party Game

Karen was planning a party. She wanted to play a guessing game. She wrote clues. Then she drew pictures. Read Karen's clues. Then draw lines to the pictures they tell about.

I'm round and orange.

You might give me a grin.

I make great pie.

Don't slip on my peel!

I'm green before I'm ripe.

I'm yellow when I'm good to eat.

I'm the color of the whitest snow.

I keep my soft fur very clean.

I drink milk and catch mice.

I have a nose. I have a tail.

If you ride on my back,

We'll trot and gallop along the trail.

I keep the sun out of your eyes.

You might wear me as you

round up a herd of cattle.

IF5610 Inferencing

Where Would You Go?

Look at each child's list. Look at the stores. Where should each child shop? Write the matching store's number on the line.

John needs:

eggs
milk
bread _____

Susie needs:

kitty litter
dog food
hamster cage _____

Juanita needs:

cold pills
cough drops
baby powder _____

Jose needs:

gum drops
lollipops
candy bars _____

Steve needs:

nails
saw
hammer _____

Karen needs:

pizza
soda
salad _____

Fruits and Vegetables

Guess what fruit or vegetable each child likes.
Draw a line to the correct picture.

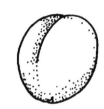

1. Jason's mother called him a rabbit when he asked for his favorite orange vegetable. What vegetable does Jason want?

2. Jody likes to pick the fruit from trees in her backyard. The round, ripe fruit has a red skin. Jody does not eat the core. What did Jody pick and eat?

3. Diane helps Grandpa dig up her favorite vegetable. It has a brown skin and eyes. She loves to eat this vegetable with gravy. What did Diane help Grandpa dig?

4. Frank loves this fuzzy, juicy fruit. Mom peels them to make his favorite pie. What fruit does Frank like best?

5. Tony picked six ears of his favorite vegetable. It grows on tall stalks. Tony will butter one before he eats it right off the cob. What did Tony pick?

Try this: What is your favorite fruit? Write two sentences that tell about it, but don't write its name.

Who Needs to Sneeze?

Look at the animals. They all have colds!

Circle Yes or No for each of the following sentences.

1. A bird with a cold would go to a nest
    to take a nap.   Yes   No

2. A whale who sneezed could make big
    waves in the water.   Yes   No

3. A rabbit eats hot soup to get over a cold.   Yes   No

4. Both the bird and the whale could use
    leaves as handkerchiefs.   Yes   No

5. A rabbit can climb a tree to sleep when
    he is ill.   Yes   No

6. A rabbit's nose wiggles all the time,
    not just when he sneezes.   Yes   No

7. A frog that coughed could shake up
    the ocean.   Yes   No

8. A whale with a cold would crawl onto
    a lily pad to rest.   Yes   No

9. Both the bird and the frog could have
    gotten sick near a pond.   Yes   No

Who Sailed the Ocean Blue in 1492?

Read the story. Then answer the questions.

In 1492, Christopher Columbus and his crew sailed from Spain across the Atlantic Ocean. They sailed on the *Niña*, the *Pinta*, and the *Santa Maria*. They wanted to find a shorter way to the Pacific Ocean and the East Indies. They did not know that a whole continent was in their way! Instead of finding gold and spices, they found a new land.

Circle the correct answers.

1. What were the *Niña*, the *Pinta*, and the *Santa Maria*?

    three men   three ships   three spices

2. What new land did Columbus find?

    Spain   North America   Canada

3. How did Columbus find the new land?

    with a map   by bumping into it

4. What was the reason for Columbus's trip?

    to find gold and spices   to find new lands

5. Which ship looks like Columbus's ship?

IF5610 Inferencing

Almost Like You!

Read to find out about bats.
Then answer the questions below.

Bats fly like birds, but they are really mammals. Bats don't have feathers. They have hair like dogs and cats. Baby bats don't hatch from eggs. They are born live. Mother bat feeds her baby milk. Bats are the only mammals that can fly. Thin skin stretched between a bat's finger bones forms wings. Bats hang upside down in caves, trees, or attics to sleep.

Match the beginning of the sentences to the endings below that tell facts you know about bats, kids, and birds.

Bats and kids

_____

_____

_____

_____

Sentence Endings
can fly.
are mammals.
are born live.
have hair.
have wings.
drink mother's milk.
live in trees.

Bats and birds

_____

_____

_____

_____

Are bats more like you or more like birds? _____

How do you know? _____

_____

As Days Grow Short

Joe watched the tail of a white and <u>charcoal</u> squirrel disappear into a hole in the trunk of a tree. Soon the furry, white and <u>gray</u> <u>mammal</u> came out and raced across the ground, <u>collecting</u> nuts. Joe knew the squirrel was <u>hoard-</u> <u>ing</u> food to eat during the cold months when snow would be covering the ground. Joe raced after the squirrel to see where he went. Joe's feet made crunching sounds in the leaves that had fallen off the trees. Joe smiled. He knew his favorite <u>season</u> would soon be here.

Think about the underlined words. Circle the best answer.

1. The white and charcoal mammal is a . . .

    squirrel.   brown bear.   rabbit.

2. Hoarding means . . .

    eating lots of food.   storing food.   giving food away.

3. The season that is coming is . . .

    winter.   fall.   spring.

4. How do you know? _____

Match the words that have almost the same meaning.

animal   gray

charcoal   storing

hoarding   season

time of year   mammal

Take-Along Home

Toby was ready to go for his morning walk. He peeked outside and looked around the yard. "Where is Sam?" Toby asked out loud. He wanted to take a nice quiet walk by himself. He didn't want that pesky Sam following him.

Slowly Toby began to walk across the grass. He was looking for bright red flowers. They were his favorite food. Then he heard "Sniff, sniff." The sound was coming closer and closer. "Oh, no!" thought Toby. "It's Sam." Toby stood very still.

But Sam found him. Sam sniffed Toby's feet. Sam licked Toby's nose. Toby didn't like that. Toby pulled his feet and head into his shell. Then Sam began to bark. Toby was happy that he was safe inside his little take-along home.

Draw a picture of Toby

Draw a picture of Sam

Circle the clues in the story that tell you about Toby.

Toby pulled his feet into his shell.

Toby listened.

Toby pulled his head into his shell.

What clues in the story tell you about Sam?

Sam sniffed.

Sam barked.

Sam wagged his tail.

What Time Is It?

Match each story to the clock that shows the correct time.
Write the letter on the line.

1. Debra had a sandwich and apple for lunch at 11 o'clock. She played outside for almost an hour. Then her mother called her inside. It was time to take their puppy to the vet. About what time was it? _____

A

2. David gets up every school day at 6:15. That gives him time to get dressed and eat breakfast. David leaves home an hour after he gets up. He walks three blocks to the bus stop. His bus comes about what time? _____

B

3. Cindy's brother's favorite TV program comes on at 7:00. It lasts for an hour. Cindy's favorite program comes on right after that. What time does Cindy's program begin? _____

C

4. Paul got home from school at 3:30. He practiced the piano for half an hour. Then his mother said he could play outside with friends. What time did Paul go out to play? _____

D

5. Diane practiced with her soccer team from 6 o'clock until 7 o'clock. Then she did homework until 8 o'clock. Mom said Diane could read for an hour before going to bed. When was Diane's bedtime? _____

E

Name _____

Recipe Fun

Chris wanted something special for lunch.
He helped Mom make it.
Chris emptied a box of red powder into a bowl.
He watched as Mom poured in one cup of boiling water.
Chris stirred the water until the powder was mixed in well.
Then Chris measured one cup of cold water.
He poured the water into the red liquid. Now all
he had to do was wait for his treat to chill!

Circle the best answer.

What did Chris and his mom make?

      ice cream   Jell-O   juice

Why was Mom the one to pour the boiling water into the bowl?

    She wanted to help Chris.   So Chris did not get burned by hot water.

What flavor did Chris probably make?

      strawberry   lime   grape

Where would Chris chill his treat?

    on the table   in the refrigerator   in the oven

Draw a line from each sentence to the correct picture.

If someone gets out bread, peanut butter,
and jelly, they are probably going to make . . .

If someone gets out ice cream, chocolate sauce,
and nuts, they are probably going to make . . .

Outdoor Fun

Read the list of sports. Write the letter of the sport each story is talking about on the blank line. You will not use all of the sports listed.

1. Angie put a sandwich, a water bottle, an apple, and a trail map in her backpack. She put on shorts and boots.
   Angie is going to go . . . ____.

2. Phil got his water bottle. He put on a helmet. He threw one leg over the bar and sat down on the seat. He checked his brakes. Then he peddled off.
   Phil is going . . . ____.

A snorkeling

B swimming

C canoeing

D snowboarding

E horseback riding

F sledding

G biking

H hiking

3. Tracy wanted to cool off. She got a towel and changed into her suit. She had to look for her goggles and nose plug. Then she put on rubber sandals.
   Tracy is going . . . ____.

4. When Juan whistled, Blaze trotted to the gate. Juan put a bridle, blanket, and saddle on Blaze. Then Juan put his foot in the stirrup.
   Juan is going . . . ____.

5. Kacie put on a life jacket, stepped into the boat, and sat down on the seat. She pushed away from the dock and dipped her paddle into the water.
   Kacie is going . . . ____.

Pets on Parade

Read all the riddles. Can you guess what pet each child has?

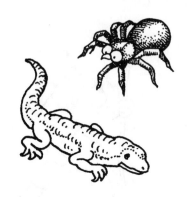

1. Joan said, "My pet's name is Polly. She has green, orange, and yellow feathers. She has a sharp beak and she can fly."

2. "My pet's name is Goldie, " said Billy. "She has big eyes and a fan-like tail. She lives in a tank. I can't hold her, but I love to look at her."

3. Marla said, "My pet has eight legs. I call him Fuzzy because he has a furry body and furry legs. Some people think my pet can poison you with a bite, but he can't!"

4. "My pet is Lizzy," said Rob. "He loves to eat insects. He's a reptile. If you pull on his tail it might fall off. But don't worry! If it does, he'll grow another."

5. Nell said, "I have a pet named Slider. Slider has no legs, just a long, skinny body. Her tongue flicks in and out. She swallows her food whole."

Use the Word Bank to complete each sentence below.

Joan's pet, Polly, is a _____ .

Billy's pet, Goldie, is a _____ .

Marla's pet, Fuzzy, is a _____ .

Rob's pet, Lizzy, is a _____ .

Nell's pet, Slider, is a _____ .

Word Bank
lizard
tarantula
fish
parrot
snake

Cookie Bandit

"Holly, why did you eat so many cookies?" asked Heather.

"I didn't," said Holly. "You must have!"

"I did not." said Heather.

Because each girl was sure the other had eaten most of the cookies, they stopped talking or playing together. Later, when Heather walked across the dining room, she almost stepped on a cookie. "What is this doing here?" she wondered. She walked down the hall and knocked on Holly's door.

"Holly! Look what I found on the floor."

"On the floor? How did it get there?" asked Holly.

"I don't know," responded Heather, "but we will find out."

The girls got four more cookies from the jar and set them out on a plate. Then they hid in the closet.

Soon Ed trotted in. He jumped up on a chair, put both front paws on the table, and picked up a cookie. He jumped down and padded out the door with his treat.

Heather and Holly laughed, "Now we know who the cookie bandit is."

Complete the following.

Who are Holly and Heather?

        friends   brothers   sisters

What clues told you who they are? _____

_____

How do they feel at the beginning of the story? _____

How do they feel at the end of the story? _____

Who is Ed?

        a little brother   a dog   a cat

What clues told you who Ed is? _____

_____

Bug Off!

Lizzie and I decided to hunt bugs. I got a jar and punched some holes in the lid. Then Lizzie and I went out to the backyard.

"Where should we look?" I asked.

Lizzie's tongue flicked out and pointed to bushes near the porch. Lizzie perched on my shoulder. We got down and crawled under the bushes. It was dark and damp. We sat very quietly, watching for bugs. I found two ants. I dropped them into the jar. "You guard the jar, Lizzie. I'll get more bugs." I found a caterpillar and put it in the jar. Then I saw a small, gray spider. It scurried away. I crawled after it, but the spider got away.

Then I checked the other bugs we'd caught, but they had all disappeared! Lizzie was sitting on the rim of the jar. I smiled and said, "Lizzie, you are a better bug catcher than I am!"

Complete the following.

1. Lizzie is a . . .

      cat.   bird.   lizard.

2. Draw a picture of Lizzie.

3. What happened to the bugs they caught?

    Lizzie ate them.   They crawled away.   Nothing.

4. How do you think the child felt when all the bugs disappeared? Why?

_____

_____

Name _____

More Bug Off!

Use the Word Bank and the clues to identify other bugs Lizzie and her owner caught. Write the bug's name on the line. Draw a picture of each bug on the jar.

Word Bank

mosquito   moth   bee
ladybug   fly   cricket

Leave a light on
for me,
and I'll
come flying.

I'm the
sweetest bug
you can catch.
But watch out
for my sting!

I don't need
a fiddle.
I make music
with my legs.

When you look
at me,
you'll see spots.

You might call me
a vampire.
I love to suck
your blood.

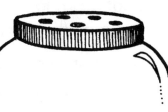

My name is the
same
as what I do.

IF5610 Inferencing

Fun in the Sun

Read the story. Circle the correct answers as you read.

1. The sand was hot under my bare feet. I ran to the water. Waves came up and wet my feet.

    A. Where am I?

   at a playground   at the beach   at a swimming pool

    B. What season is it?

   fall   winter   summer

2. I sat down on some big rocks. The rocks made a little pool. I saw a starfish there. Three little crabs crawled underwater. I tried to pick one up, but it snapped at me.

    A. Where did the water in the pool come from?

   from a hose   from rain   from the sea

    B. What did the crab use to snap?

   its shell   its claw   its teeth

3. I saw my friend Margie. She was busy building something out of sand. I sat down to help her. We built towers and a moat. But when the tide came in, the whole thing fell apart.

    A. What kind of building was it?

   a sand castle   a cabin   a school

    B. What did the tide do to the building?

   carried it to the beach   washed it away

Bath Time

Tyler got the shampoo. Holly found a towel. Holly pulled the tub into the yard. Tyler filled it with water.

"Here, Dusty," Holly called.

Dusty raced across the yard. When he saw the tub, his tail drooped. Dusty lay down and rolled over.

"Help me, Tyler," said Holly.

The kids carried Dusty to the tub. Tyler shampooed Dusty while Holly held him.

"Time to rinse off the soap," said Tyler. Just then, Dusty shook. Soap suds flew everywhere. Holly and Tyler were now covered with soap, too.

Circle the correct answers.

1. Tyler and Holly gave Dusty a . . .

        towel.   tub.   bath.

2. Dusty is a . . .

        cat.   dog.   brother.

Answer these questions.

3. How did you know what Dusty is?

_____

4. What did Tyler and Holly need to do when they finished?

_____

5. Why do you think Dusty lay down when he saw the tub of water?

_____

 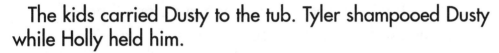

Where's Joey?

"I'm back," Mom called as she came in the back door and set two bags on the kitchen table. Samantha put down her book and went to see if she could help Mom. Samantha put cans of soup, beans, and corn away. Mom put milk, eggs, and lunch meat in the refrigerator.

"Where's Joey?" Mom asked.

"I don't know," said Samantha. "I'll check his room." Joey wasn't there. She looked carefully around the room. Joey's glove, bat, and team cap were gone. Samantha ran to the garage. Joey's bike was gone, too. She went back into the kitchen.

"Joey's not here, Mom. I think I know where he is." She looked at the calendar. Now she was sure. "Joey's at baseball practice," she told Mom.

Answer the questions.

1. Where had Mom been? _____

2. How do you know? _____

3. Who is Joey? _____

4. How do you know? _____

5. How did Samantha know Joey was at baseball practice? _____

   _____

6. Why do you think Samantha looked at the calendar? _____

   _____

Kids Dig In!

Marsha and Tim want to plant gardens. They went to a store to buy what they needed for their gardens.

Here are Marsha's seeds:

Here are Tim's seeds:

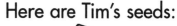

Circle the correct answers.

1. Aunt Susie asked if she could plant beans. Whose garden would she plant them in?

    Marsha's   Tim's

2. What will Marsha be able to make from her garden?

    soup   a bouquet   a basket

3. What will Tim be able to make from his garden?

    a basket   bread   a salad

4. Whose garden will the rabbits like better?

    Marsha's   Tim's

5. Which kind of seeds is Marsha growing that birds and kids like to eat?

    zinnia   petunia   sunflower

6. Circle the tools that Marsha and Tim will need.

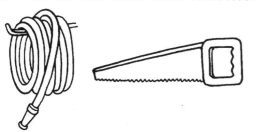

Good Day, Bad Day

Tyler jumped out of bed shouting, "Today is my birthday!" He hurried downstairs. Everyone was eating breakfast already.

"Good morning, Tyler," said Dad.

Mom gave him a hug. "What would you like for breakfast?"

"Can I have toaster waffles?" he asked. Mom nodded yes.

His sister Cindy kept eating her breakfast.

Tyler frowned. Had everyone forgotten his birthday? He sat down. "Where's Sparky?" Sparky always sat right beside him.

"Wasn't she in your room?" Cindy asked.

"I haven't seen her," said Mom.

"Oh, no," Tyler thought. "What if something has happened to Sparky?

"Why don't you call her?" asked Dad.

"Sparky. Here, Sparky!" Sparky didn't come, but Tyler heard a scratch at the door. When he opened the door, there was Sparky. She had a balloon tied to her collar. And Tyler's two best friends were there holding gifts. "Surprise!"

Circle the best answers.

1. How did Tyler feel when he woke up?

   excited   worried   lonely

2. Why didn't his family wish him a happy birthday?

   They forgot his birthday.   It wasn't his birthday.

   They wanted to surprise him.   Sparky was lost.

3. How did he feel when no one knew where Sparky was?

   happy   lonely   worried

4. What kind of day is Tyler probably going to have?

   good day   bad day

Draw a picture of the balloon tied to Sparky.

Don't Get Lost

Joan was going to Nell's house for the first time. She carefully read the directions.

> Walk three blocks from school. On the corner is a large church and a house with yellow shutters. Go around the corner and look for my house. It is green and has a big tree in the front yard. The house number is 453.

Joan frowned. She looked up and down the street in front of the school.

1. What did Nell forget to tell Joan? _____

   _____

   Joan decided to walk west along the street. She walked three blocks. There was a white house with a green roof, an empty lot, and a trailer on this corner.

2. Was Joan at the right corner? _____

3. How do you know? _____

   _____

   Joan walked back to her school and tried the other direction. After walking two blocks she came to a corner with a large church and a house with yellow shutters.

4. What should Joan do now? _____

   Joan turned the corner and began looking for a green house with a big tree in front. There were two green houses with trees. Joan stopped at the first one, then walked up and knocked on Nell's front door.

5. How did Joan know this was Nell's house? _____

   _____

Homework Trouble

Brad sat at his desk to do his homework. He added up some numbers. Then he took a break to play with his pet, Sammy. He rubbed Sammy's white fur and tickled his pink tail. While Brad worked, Sammy stretched his paw through the wire cage and tugged at Brad's paper.

"No, Sammy," Brad said. "This is my homework. You can't play with it." Instead he gave Sammy a tissue. Sammy squeaked as he pulled the tissue into his cage. He shredded it and made a new nest.

When Brad finished his homework, he left his paper on the desk and went to watch his favorite TV show. At bedtime, he decided to put his paper and book in his backpack. But his paper was gone, except for one tiny scrap. "Oh, no!" Brad moaned.

Answer each question with a complete sentence.

1. What kind of homework was Brad doing? _____

2. What happened to Brad's paper? _____

    _____

3. What should Brad do now? _____

    _____

4. How do you think Brad felt? _____

    _____

5. What kind of pet is Sammy? _____

Letter to Grandma

Dear Grandma,

When I woke up this morning at nine o'clock, I thought I had missed the bus. Then I looked outside. Guess what happened while I was sleeping?

After breakfast I put on the gift you gave me for my birthday. I also put on mittens, a hat, and a jacket. Then I went outside.

I made tracks in the yard. I looked at the hill by our house, and I got a great idea. I ran to the garage. Soon I was coasting down the hill. What a day!

Love,
Jake

Answer each question with a complete sentence.

1. What happened while Jake was sleeping? _____

   _____

2. Why wasn't Jake late for school? _____

   _____

3. What did Jake get out of the garage? _____

   _____

4. How do you think Jake felt about his day? _____

   _____

5. Circle Grandma's gift to Jake.

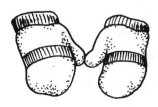

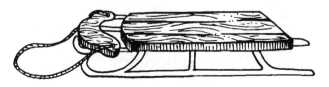

Troubles

"Mom, may I go with Amy to the movie today?" Jill asked.

"Yes," said Mom.

"Oh, boy! Today is going to be a great day," Jill said. Her mom gave her money to buy popcorn. Jill put it in her coat pocket and ran all the way to Amy's house.

Amy's mother bought tickets for both girls. Amy and Jill went to buy popcorn, but when Jill reached into her pocket for her money it was gone. Instead, she found a hole in her pocket.

After the movie, the two girls walked to Amy's house. It was four o'clock when they got there. "I can stay until five o'clock," Jill told her friend. "Mom wants me home to help with supper."

The two girls decided to eat some cookies and play a game. Jill forgot to watch the time. When she heard the phone ring, she looked at the clock. "Oh, no!" she moaned. "I bet that's Mom." She jumped up and knocked the cookie plate off the table. The plate broke. Jill's mouth quivered as she looked at the mess. "I'm sorry," she whispered.

Answer each question with a complete sentence.

1. How did Jill feel at the beginning of the story? _____

_____

2. What happened to Jill's popcorn money? _____

_____

3. Why did Jill think it was her mom on the phone? _____

_____

4. How did Jill feel when she broke the plate? _____

5. Circle the answer that best tells how Jill probably felt about her day.

    It was a bad day.   It was a boring day.   It was a great day.

Way Out West

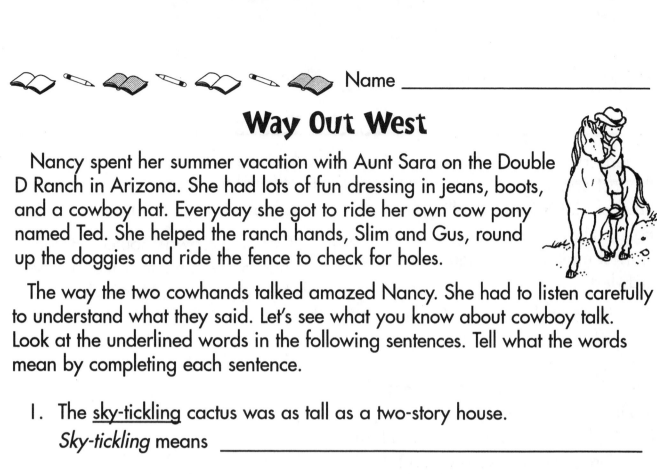

Nancy spent her summer vacation with Aunt Sara on the Double D Ranch in Arizona. She had lots of fun dressing in jeans, boots, and a cowboy hat. Everyday she got to ride her own cow pony named Ted. She helped the ranch hands, Slim and Gus, round up the doggies and ride the fence to check for holes.

The way the two cowhands talked amazed Nancy. She had to listen carefully to understand what they said. Let's see what you know about cowboy talk. Look at the underlined words in the following sentences. Tell what the words mean by completing each sentence.

1. The <u>sky-tickling</u> cactus was as tall as a two-story house.
    Sky-tickling means _____

2. I had never ridden a horse before. I paced back and forth while Gus saddled Ted. Gus told me that Ted was gentle, and that there was no reason to act <u>like a long-tailed cat in a room full of rocking chairs</u>.
    Long-tailed cat in a room full of rocking chairs means _____

    _____

3. Everyone laughed when Slim said that my brother knew how to have a <u>Texas-sized tantrum</u>.
    Texas-sized tantrum means _____

4. When Ted disappeared from the corral one morning, I couldn't go riding. Slim tried to cheer me up because I felt <u>as low as a snake's belly</u>.
    As low as a snake's belly means _____

    _____

5. When I heard one of the hands had found Ted, I took off for the corral <u>like a scalded cat</u>. Now I could ride again!
    Like a scalded cat means _____

    _____

Off to the Races

Herbert was tired of always being the last one to get anywhere. He was tired of all his friends calling him Pokey. He was especially tired of Harriet making fun of the way he crawled along.

So Herbert decided to do something about it. He decided to practice running. He drew a line in the dirt with his front toes. He stood behind the line. He said to himself, "Ready. Set. Go!" Herbert practiced sprinting over the line and racing down the path. "It sure would be a lot easier if I didn't have to carry this old shell around on my back," Herbert muttered. But he didn't quit. He kept practicing.

So the next time, Herbert was ready when Harriet said, "Herbert, all you do is crawl along."

"I challenge you to a race," he said.

Harriet hopped up and down laughing. "It won't be a race," she said. "I know I'll win, paws down."

"We'll just see about that," said Herbert.

The next morning, with all their friends gathered for the race, Herbert and Harriet lined up side by side. Harriet was still laughing. Herbert clamped his jaws together and looked down the trail.

"Go!" the crowd shouted. Herbert pushed off with his four feet. He was off to a great start. Harriet fell behind. But that only lasted a moment. Soon Harriet bounced past Herbert.

"You are so pokey," she yelled back.

Herbert watched her race away and out of sight. At first he felt like hiding his head in his shell. But he kept going as fast as he could. After a few minutes, he spotted Harriet. She was sitting under a tree, nibbling a carrot.

As Herbert hurried by her, Harriet yelled, "You go ahead. I'll catch up after I finish my snack."

Herbert kept going. He could see the finish line. All their friends were waiting to see who would win. Herbert remembered all the things he'd practiced as he sprinted for the line. He knew Harriet was close behind. He lunged forward.

"Herbert is the winner!" yelled all his friends. "Hurray for Herbert!"

Off to the Races (cont.)

Draw a picture of Herbert.

[ ]

List 2 clues that told you about Herbert.

_____

_____

_____

Draw a picture of Harriet.

[ ]

List 2 clues that told you about Harriet.

_____

_____

_____

Complete the following.

1. What is another name for this story?

_____

2. How do you think Herbert felt when his friends called him Pokey?

_____

3. Why did Herbert feel like hiding his head in his shell?

_____

_____

4. How did all of Herbert's friends feel when he won the race?

_____

5. How do you think Harriet felt when Herbert won the race?

_____

Answer Key
Grades 1–2

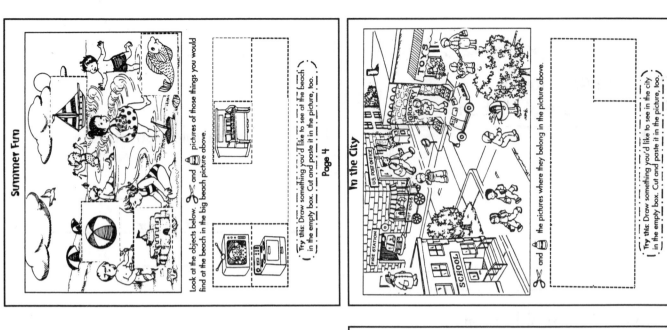

Summer Fun

Look at the objects below. ✂ and 📋 pictures of those things you would find at the beach in the big beach picture above.

Try this: Draw something you'd like to see at the beach in the empty box. Cut and paste it in the picture, too.

Page 4

In the City

✂ and 📋 the pictures where they belong in the picture above.

Try this: Draw something you'd like to see in the city in the empty box. Cut and paste it in the picture, too.

Page 7

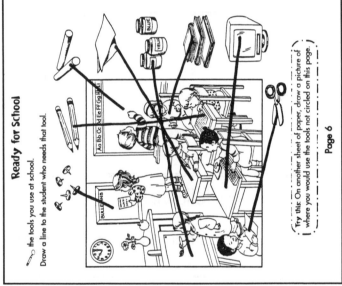

Ready for School

✏ the tools you use at school.
Draw a line to the student who needs that tool.

Try this: On another sheet of paper, draw a picture of where you would use the tools not circled on this page.

Page 6

What's Wrong with This Picture?

Look at the picture. ✂ the things that don't belong.

Try this: Draw a picture of your school room. Put four things in the picture that don't belong at school.

Page 5

Toy Swap

Draw a line from each child to the toy he or she would like.

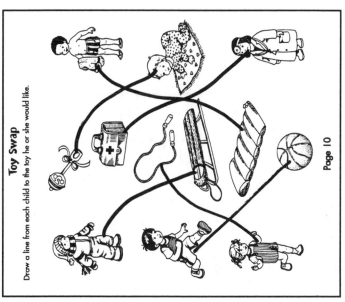

Page 10

What Rhymes?

Read each list of words. Then read the sentence. Circle the rhyming word that belongs in the sentence.

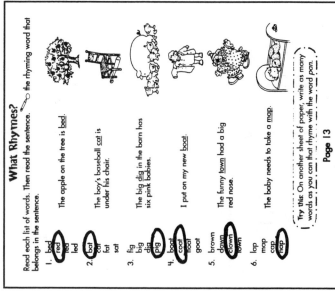

1. bed
   red
   led

The apple on the tree is red.

2. bat
   cat
   fat
   sat

The boy's baseball cat is under his chair.

3. fig
   big
   pig

The big dig in the barn has six pink babies.

4. boat
   coat
   float

I put on my new boat.

5. brown
   clown
   town

The funny town had a big red nose.

6. lap
   mop
   cap
   nap

The baby needs to take a nap.

Try this: On another sheet of paper, write as many words as you can that rhyme with the word pan.

Page 13

At the Airport

What would you find at the airport? Cut and paste those pictures that belong in the airport scene above.

Try this: Draw something you'd like to see of the airport in the empty boxes. Cut and paste them in the picture, too.

Page 9

What Comes Next?

Look at the pictures. Draw a picture that shows what happens next.

Illustrations will very.

Page 12

In the Country

Circle the things that don't belong in the picture. Underline the farm animal families below.

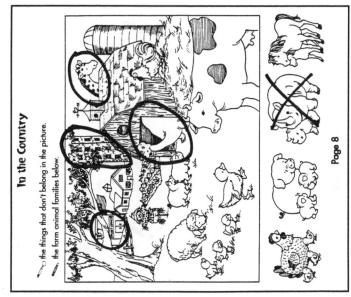

Page 8

What's Happening?

Look at the pictures in each row. Circle the picture on the right that shows what happens next.

Underline the picture above that gave you clues about what the boy was making.

Underline the picture that gave you clues about what animal was being fed.

Underline the picture that gave you clues about what plant would grow.

Page 11

Where Would You Go?

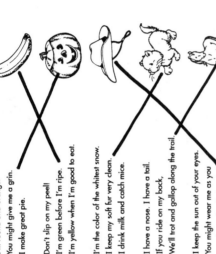

Look at each child's list. Look at the stores. Where should each child shop?
Write the matching store's number on the line.

John needs:
eggs
milk
bread   **3**

Juanita needs:
cold pills
cough drops
baby powder   **6**

Steve needs:
nails
saw
hammer   **1**

Susie needs:
kitty litter
dog food
hamster cage   **5**

Jose needs:
gum drops
lollipops
candy bars   **4**

Karen needs:
pizza
soda
salad   **2**

Page 16

Who Sailed the Ocean Blue in 1492?

Read the story. Then answer the questions.

In 1492, Christopher Columbus and his crew sailed from Spain across the Atlantic Ocean. They sailed on the *Niña*, the *Pinta*, and the *Santa Maria*. They wanted to find a shorter way to the Pacific Ocean and the East Indies. They did not know that a whole continent was in their way! Instead of finding gold and spices, they found a new land.

Circle the correct answers.

1. What were the *Niña*, the *Pinta*, and the *Santa Maria*?
   three men   (three ships)   three spices

2. What new land did Columbus find?
   (North America)   Spain   Canada

3. How did Columbus find the new land?
   with a map   (by bumping into it)

4. What was the reason for Columbus's trip?
   (to find gold and spices)   to find new lands

5. Which ship looks like Columbus's ship?

Page 19

Party Game

Karen was planning a party. She wanted to play a guessing game. She wrote clues. Then she drew pictures. Read Karen's clues. Then draw lines to the pictures they tell about.

I'm round and orange.
You might give me a grin.
I make great pie.

Don't slip on my peel!
I'm green before I'm ripe.
I'm yellow when I'm good to eat.

I'm the color of the whitest snow.
I keep my soft fur very clean.
I drink milk and catch mice.

I have a nose. I have a tail.
If you ride on my back,
We'll trot and gallop along the trail.

I keep the sun out of your eyes.
You might wear me as you
round up a herd of cattle.

Page 15

Who Needs to Sneeze?

Look at the animals. They all have colds!

Circle Yes or No for each of the following sentences.

1. A bird with a cold would go to a nest to take a nap.   Yes   **No**

2. A whale who sneezed could make big waves in the water.   **Yes**   No

3. A rabbit eats hot soup to get over a cold.   Yes   **No**

4. Both the bird and the whale could use leaves as handkerchiefs.   Yes   **No**

5. A rabbit can climb a tree to sleep when he is ill.   Yes   **No**

6. A rabbit's nose wiggles all the time, not just when he sneezes.   **Yes**   No

7. A frog that coughed could shake up the ocean.   Yes   **No**

8. A whale with a cold would crawl unto a lily pad to rest.   Yes   **No**

9. Both the bird and the frog could have gotten sick near a pond.   **Yes**   No

Page 18

Where Am I?

Read each story. Answer the questions.

1. Stacie rode the merry-go-round. She bought a ticket for a ride on the ferris wheel. Then she rode the roller coaster.
   Where is Stacie? _Amusement park_

2. Paul saw the polar bears and the lion. He watched the monkeys and the gorilla. Then he walked slowly through the reptile house.
   Where is Paul? _at the zoo_

3. Tina walked in the door and hung up her coat. She sat down at her desk, got out her book and began to read. She read until she was told to put her book away. Then she got ready for her spelling test.
   Where is Tina? _at school_

4. Karen ran to the barn to see the cows, sheep, chickens, and pony. She was always glad to visit Grandma and Grandpa. She loved to run in the fields, gather the eggs, and ride on the tractor.
   Where do Karen's grandparents live? _on a farm_

5. Tony followed Mom through the big door. First he saw men's shirts and shoes. They walked past the pants and socks. Then Tony saw racks of dresses. They went to the second floor and found clothes for kids.
   Where are Tony and his mom? _clothing store (mall)_

Page 14

Fruits and Vegetables

Guess what fruit or vegetable each child likes.
Draw a line to the correct picture.

1. Jason's mother called him a rabbit when he asked for his favorite orange vegetable. What vegetable does Jason want?

2. Jody likes to pick the fruit from trees in her backyard. The round, ripe fruit has a red skin. Jody does not eat the core. What did Jody pick and eat?

3. Diane helps Grandpa dig up her favorite vegetable. It has a brown skin and eyes. She loves to eat this vegetable with gravy. What did Diane help Grandpa dig?

4. Frank loves this fuzzy, juicy fruit. Mom peels them to make his favorite pie. What fruit does Frank like best?

5. Tony picked six ears of his favorite vegetable. It grows on tall stalks. Tony will butter one before he eats it right off the cob. What did Tony pick?

Try this: What is your favorite fruit? Write two sentences that tell about it, but don't write its name.

Page 17

Almost Like You!

Read to find out about bats.
Then answer the questions below.

Bats fly like birds, but they are really mammals. Bats don't have feathers. They have hair like dogs and cats. Baby bats don't hatch from eggs. They are born live. Mother bat feeds her baby milk. Bats are the only mammals that can fly. Thin skin stretched between a bat's finger bones forms wings. Bats hang upside down in caves, trees, or attics to sleep.

Match the beginning of the sentences to the endings below that tell facts you know about bats, kids, and birds.

Sentence Endings
can fly.
are mammals.
are born live.
have hair.
have wings.
drink mother's milk.
live in trees.

Bats and kids: mammals, born live, have hair, drink milk

Bats and birds: can fly, have wings, live in trees

Are bats more like you or more like birds? They are like me
How do you grow? in four ways. (Answers will vary)

Page 20

As Days Grow Short

Joe watched the tail of a white and <u>charcoal</u> squirrel disappear into a hole in the trunk of a tree. Soon the furry, white and <u>gray</u> <u>mammal</u> came out and raced across the ground, collecting nuts. Joe knew the squirrel was <u>hoarding</u> food to eat during the cold months when snow would be covering the ground. Joe raced after the squirrel to see where he went. Joe's feet made crunching sounds in the leaves that had fallen off the trees. Joe smiled. He knew his favorite <u>season</u> would soon be here.

Think about the underlined words. Circle the best answer.

1. The white and charcoal mammal is a . . . .
(squirrel.) brown bear. rabbit.

2. Hoarding means . . . .
(storing food.) eating lots of food. giving food away.

3. The season that is coming is . . . .
(winter.) fall. spring.

4. How do you know? Leaves falling, squirrel collecting nuts

Match the words that have almost the same meaning.
animal — gray
charcoal — storing
hoarding — season
time of year — mammal

Page 21

Take-Along Home

Toby was ready to go for his morning walk. He peeked outside and looked around the yard. "Where is Sam?" Toby asked out loud. "Where is Sam?" Toby wanted to take a nice quiet walk by himself. He didn't want that pesky Sam following him.

Slowly Toby began to walk across the grass. He was looking for bright red flowers. They were his favorite food. Then he heard "Sniff, sniff." The sound was coming closer and closer. "Oh, no!" thought Toby. "It's Sam." Toby stood very still.

But Sam found him. Sam sniffed Toby's feet. Sam licked Toby's nose. Toby didn't like that. Toby pulled his feet and head into his shell. Then Sam began to bark. Toby knew that he was safe inside his little take-along home.

Draw a picture of Toby [Picture of a turtle.]

Draw a picture of Sam [Picture of a dog.]

Circle the clues in the story that tell you about Toby.
(Toby pulled his head into his shell.)
Toby listened.
(Toby pulled his feet into his shell.)
Sam wagged his tail.

What clues in the story tell you about Sam?
(Sam barked.)
(Sam sniffed.)

Page 22

What Time Is It?

A   B   C   D   E

Match each story to the clock that shows the correct time. Write the letter on the line.

1. Debra had a sandwich and apple for lunch at 11 o'clock. She played outside for almost an hour. Then her mother called her inside. It was time to take their puppy to the vet. About what time was it? E

2. David gets up every school day at 6:15. That gives him time to get dressed and eat breakfast. David leaves home an hour after he gets up. His bus comes about what time? A

3. Cindy's brother's favorite TV program comes on at 7:00. It lasts for an hour. Cindy's favorite program comes on right after that. What time does Cindy's program begin? B

4. Paul got home from school at 3:30. He practiced the piano for half an hour. Then his mother said he could play outside with friends. What time did Paul go out to play? D

5. Diane practiced with her soccer team from 6 o'clock until 7 o'clock. Then she did homework until 8 o'clock. Mom said Diane could read for an hour before going to bed. When was Diane's bedtime? C

Page 23

Recipe Fun

Chris wanted something special for lunch.
He helped Mom make it.
Chris emptied a box of red powder into a bowl. He watched as Mom poured in one cup of boiling water. Chris stirred the water until the powder was mixed in well. Then Chris measured one cup of cold water. He poured the water into the red liquid. Now all he had to do was wait for his treat to chill.

Circle the best answer.

What did Chris and his mom make?
ice cream (jello) juice

Why was Mom the one to pour the boiling water into the bowl?
(So Chris did not get burned by hot water.)

What flavor did Chris probably make?
(strawberry) lime grape

Where would Chris chill his treat?
on the table (in the refrigerator) in the oven

Draw a line from each sentence to the correct picture.
If someone gets out bread, peanut butter, and jelly, they are probably going to make . . .
If someone gets out ice cream, chocolate syrup, and nuts, they are probably going to make . . .

Page 24

Outdoor Fun

Read the list of sports. Write the letter of the sport each story is talking about on the blank line. You will not use all of the sports listed.

A snorkeling
B swimming
C canoeing
D snowboarding
E horseback riding
F sledding
G biking
H hiking

1. Angie put a sandwich, a water bottle, an apple, and a trail map in her backpack. She put on shorts and boots. Angie is going to go . . . H

2. Phil got his water bottle. He put on a helmet. He threw one leg over the bar and sat down on the seat. He checked his brakes. Then he pedalled off. Phil is going . . . G

3. Tracy wanted to cool off. She got a towel and changed into her suit. She had to look for her goggles and nose plug. Then she put on rubber sandals. Tracy is going . . . B

4. When Juan whistled, Blaze trotted to the gate. Juan put a bridle, blanket, and saddle on Blaze. Then Juan put his foot in the stirrup. Juan is going . . . E

5. Kacie put on a life jacket, stepped into the boat, and sat down on the seat. She pushed away from the dock and dipped her paddle into the water. Kacie is going . . . C

Page 25

Bug Off!

Lizzie and I decided to hunt bugs. I got a jar and punched some holes in the lid. Then Lizzie and I went out to the backyard.

"Where should we look?" I asked.

Lizzie's tongue flicked out and pointed to bushes near the porch. Lizzie perched on my shoulder. We got down and crawled under the bushes. It was dark and damp. We sat very quietly, watching for bugs. I found two ants. I dropped them into the jar. "You guard the jar, Lizzie, I'll get more bugs." I found a caterpillar and put it in the jar. The I saw a small, gray spider. It scurried away. I crawled after it, but the spider got away.

Then I checked the other bugs we'd caught, but they had all disappeared! Lizzie was sitting on the rim of the jar. I smiled and said, "Lizzie, you are a better bug catcher than I am!"

Complete the following.

1. Lizzie is a . . . .

   cat.   bird.   (lizard)

2. Draw a picture of Lizzie.

3. What happened to the bugs they caught?

   (Lizzie ate them.)   They crawled away.   Nothing.

4. How do you think the child felt when all the bugs disappeared? Why? Sad, because Lizzie ate a good meal or- Sad, because he wanted to look at bugs.

Page 28

Bath Time

Tyler got the shampoo. Holly found a towel. Holly pulled the tub into the yard. Tyler filled it with water.

"Here, Dusty," Holly called.

Dusty raced across the yard. When he saw the tub, his tail dropped. Dusty lay down and rolled over.

"Help me, Tyler," said Holly.

The kids carried Dusty to the tub. Tyler shampooed Dusty while Holly held him.

"Time to rinse off the soap," said Tyler. Just then, Dusty shook. Soap suds flew everywhere. Holly and Tyler were now covered with soap, too.

Circle the correct answers.

1. Tyler and Holly gave Dusty a . . . .

   towel.   (bath.)   cat.

2. Dusty is a . . . .

   (dog)   brother.

Answer these questions.

3. How did you know what Dusty is? He lay down + rolled over; tail dropped

4. What did Tyler and Holly need to do when they finished? Put on dry clothes—reasonable answers

5. Why do you think Dusty lay down when he saw the tub of water? He didn't want to take a bath.

Page 31

Cookie Bandit

"Holly, why did you eat so many cookies?" asked Heather.

"I didn't," said Holly. "You must have!"

"I did not," said Heather.

Because each girl was sure the other had eaten most of the cookies, they stopped talking or playing together. Later, when Heather walked across the dining room, she almost stepped on a cookie. "What is this doing here?" she wondered. She walked down the hall and knocked on Holly's door.

"Holly! Look what I found on the floor."

"On the floor? How did it get there?" asked Holly.

"I don't know," responded Heather, "but we will find out."

The girls got four more cookies from the jar and set them out on a plate. Then they hid in the closet.

Soon Ed trotted in. He jumped up on a chair, put both front paws on the table, and picked up a cookie. He jumped down and padded out the door with his treat.

Heather and Holly laughed, "Now we know who the cookie bandit is."

Complete the following.

Who are Holly and Heather?

   friends   brothers   (sisters)

What clues told you who they are? They had rooms down the hall from one another; they live in the same house.

How do they feel at the beginning of the story? angry

How do they feel at the end of the story? happy/friends again

Who is Ed?

   (a dog)   a cat   a little brother

What clues told you who Ed is? He put his paws on the table; padded out the door.

Page 27

Fun in the Sun

Read the story. Circle the correct answers as you read.

1. The sand was hot under my bare feet. I ran to the water. Waves came up and wet my feet.

   A. Where am I?

      (at the beach)   at a playground   at a swimming pool

   B. What season is it?

      (summer)   winter   fall

2. I sat down on some big rocks. The rocks made a little pool. I saw a starfish there. Three little crabs crawled underwater. I tried to pick one up, but it snapped at me.

   A. Where did the water in the pool come from?

      (from the sea)   from rain   from a hose

   B. What did the crab use to snap?

      its shell   (its claw)   its teeth

3. I saw my friend Margie. She was busy building something out of sand. I sat down to help her. We built towers and a moat. But when the tide came in, the whole thing fell apart.

   A. What kind of building was it?

      (a sand castle)   a cabin   a school

   B. What did the tide do to the building?

      (washed it away)   carried it to the beach

Page 30

Pets on Parade

Read all the riddles. Can you guess what pet each child has?

1. Joan said, "My pet's name is Polly. She is green, orange, and yellow feathers. She has a sharp beak and she can fly."

2. "My pet's name is Goldie," said Billy. "She has big eyes and a fan-like tail. She lives in a tank. I can't hold her, but I love to look at her."

3. Marla said, "My pet has eight legs. I call him Fuzzy because he has a furry body and furry legs. Some people think my pet can poison you with a bite, but he can't!"

4. "My pet is Lizzy," said Rob. "He's a reptile. If you pull on his tail it might fall off. But don't worry! If it does, he'll grow another."

5. Nell said, "I have a pet named Slider. Slider has no legs, just a long, skinny body. Her tongue flicks in and out. She swallows her food whole."

Use the Word Bank to complete each sentence below.

Joan's pet, Polly, is a parrot.

Billy's pet, Goldie, is a fish.

Marla's pet, Fuzzy, is a tarantula.

Rob's pet, Lizzy, is a lizard.

Nell's pet, Slider, is a snake.

Word Bank
lizard
tarantula
fish
parrot
snake

Page 26

More Bug Off!

Use the Word Bank and the clues to identify other bugs Lizzie and her owner caught. Write the bug's name on the line. Draw a picture of each bug on the jar.

Word Bank
mosquito   moth   bee
ladybug   fly   cricket

Illustrations will vary.

"Leave a light on for me and I'll come flying." moth

"I'm the sweetest bug you can catch. But watch out for my sting!" bee

"I don't need a fiddle. I make music with my legs." cricket

"When you look at me, you'll see spots." ladybug

"You might call me a vampire. I love to suck your blood." mosquito

"My name is the same as what I do." fly

Page 29

Where's Joey?

"I'm back," Mom called, as she came in the back door and set two bags on the kitchen table. Samantha put her book down her book and went to see if she could help Mom. Samantha put cans of soup, beans, and corn away. Mom put milk, eggs, and lunch meat in the refrigerator.

"Where's Joey?" Mom asked.

"I don't know," said Samantha. "I'll check his room." Joey wasn't in there. She looked carefully around the room. Joey's bike was gone, too. She went back into the kitchen.

"Joey's not here, Mom. I know where he is." She looked at the calendar. Now she was sure. "Joey's at baseball practice," she told Mom.

Answer the questions.

1. Where had Mom been? at the grocery store
2. How do you know? Brought home cans of food
3. Who is Joey? Samantha's brother
4. How do you know? She went to Joey's room to check for Mom.
5. How did Samantha know Joey was at baseball practice? His glove, bat, and cap were gone.
6. Why do you think Samantha looked at the calendar? Games and practices were probably written on it.

Page 32

Kids Dig In!

Marsha and Tim want to plant gardens. They went to a store to buy what they needed for their gardens.

Here are Marsha's seeds:

Here are Tim's seeds:

Circle the correct answers.

1. Aunt Susie asked if she could plant beans. Whose garden would she plant them in? **Tim's** / Marsha's
2. What will Marsha be able to make from her garden? **a bouquet** / a basket / soup
3. What will Tim be able to make from his garden? a basket / bread / **a salad**
4. Which garden will the rabbits like better? Marsha's / **Tim's**
5. Which kind of seeds is Marsha growing that birds and kids like to eat? zinnia / petunia / **sunflower**
6. Circle the tools that Marsha and Tim will need.

Page 33

Good Day, Bad Day

Tyler jumped out of bed shouting, "Today is my birthday!" He hurried downstairs. Everyone was eating breakfast already.

"Good morning, Tyler," said Dad.

Mom gave him a hug. "What would you like for breakfast?"

"Can I have toaster waffles?" he asked. Mom nodded yes. His sister Cindy kept eating her breakfast.

Tyler frowned. Had everyone forgotten his birthday? He sat down. "Where's Sparky? Sparky always sat right beside him.

"Wasn't she in your room?" Cindy asked.

"I haven't seen her," said Mom.

"Oh, no," Tyler thought. "What if something has happened to Sparky?

"Why don't you call her?" asked Dad.

"Sparky. Here, Sparky!" Sparky didn't come, but Tyler heard a scratch at the door. When he opened the door, there was Sparky. She had a balloon tied to her collar. And Tyler's two best friends were there holding gifts. "Surprise!

Circle the best answers.

1. How did Tyler feel when he woke up?
   excited / worried / lonely
2. Why didn't his family wish him a happy birthday?
   They forgot his birthday. It wasn't his birthday.
   They wanted to surprise him.
3. How did Tyler feel when no one knew where Sparky was?
   happy / lonely / **worried**
4. What kind of day is Tyler probably going to have?
   good day / bad day

Page 34

Draw a picture of the balloon tied to Sparky.

Pictures will vary.

Don't Get Lost

Joan was going to Nell's house for the first time. She carefully read the directions.

Walk three blocks from school. On the corner is a large church and a house with yellow shutters. Go around the corner and look for my house. It is a white house with a green roof. It is the corner, and has a big tree in the front yard. The house number is 453.

Joan frowned. She looked up and down the street in front of the school.

Joan decided to walk west along the street. She walked three blocks. There was a white house with a green roof, an empty lot, and a trailer on this corner.

Joan walked back to her school and tried the other direction. After walking two blocks she came to a corner with a church and a house with yellow shutters.

Joan turned the corner and began looking for a green house with a big tree in front. There were two green houses with trees. Joan stopped at the first one, then walked up and knocked on Nell's front door.

1. What did Nell forget to tell Joan? Which direction to walk from school
2. Was Joan on the right corner? No
3. How do you know? There was no church or house with yellow shutters.
4. What should Joan do now? Go around the corner
5. How did Joan know this was Nell's house? She looked for number 453.

Page 35

Homework Trouble

Brad sat at his desk to do his homework. Then he took a break to play with his pet, Sammy. He rubbed Sammy's white fur and tickled his pink tail. While Brad worked, Sammy stretched his paw through the wire cage and tugged at Brad's paper.

"No, Sammy," Brad said. "This is my homework. You can't play with it." Instead he gave Sammy a tissue. Sammy squeaked as he pulled the tissue into his cage. He shredded it and made a new nest.

When Brad finished his homework, he left his paper on the desk and went to watch his favorite TV show. At bedtime, he decided to put his paper and book in his backpack. But his paper was gone, except for one tiny scrap. "Oh, no!" Brad moaned.

Answer each question with a complete sentence.

1. What kind of homework was Brad doing? Math
2. What happened to Brad's paper? Sammy ate it or made another nest.
3. What should Brad do now? Do his home- work again.
4. How do you think Brad felt? Probably sad and maybe angry.
5. What kind of pet is Sammy? a white mouse or rat

Page 36

Letter to Grandma

Dear Grandma,

When I woke up this morning at nine o'clock, I thought I had missed the bus. Then I looked outside. Guess what happened while I was sleeping?

After breakfast I put on the gift you gave me for my birthday. I also put on mittens, a hat, and a jacket. Then I went outside.

I made tracks in the yard. I looked at the hill by our house, and I got a great idea. I ran to the garage. Soon I was coasting down the hill. What a day!

Love,
Jake

Answer each question with a complete sentence.

1. What happened that Jake was sleeping? It snowed a lot last night.
2. Why wasn't Jake late for school? School had been cancelled.
3. What did Jake get out of the garage? Jake took out his sled.
4. How do you think Jake felt about his day? He thought this day was a lot of fun.
5. Circle Grandma's gift to Jake.

Page 37

Way Out West

Nancy spent her summer vacation with Aunt Sara on the Double D Ranch in Arizona. She had lots of fun dressing in jeans, boots, and a cowboy hat. Everyday she got to ride her own cow pony named Ted. She helped the ranch hands, Slim and Gus, round up the doggies and ride the fence to check for holes.

The way the two cowhands talked amazed Nancy. She had to listen carefully to understand what they said. Let's see what you know about cowboy talk. Look at the underlined words in the following sentences. Tell what the words mean by completing each sentence.

1. The sky-tickling cactus was as tall as a two-story house.
Sky-tickling means _very tall._

2. I had never ridden a horse before. I paced back and forth while Gus saddled Ted. Gus told me that Ted was gentle, and that there was no reason to act like a long-tailed cat in a room full of rocking chairs. Long-tailed cat in a room full of rocking chairs means _nervous about getting on the horse._

3. Everyone laughed when Slim said that my brother knew how to have a Texas-sized tantrum. Texas-sized tantrum means _very big tantrum._

4. When Ted disappeared from the corral one morning, I couldn't go riding. Slim tried to cheer me up because I felt as low as a snake's belly. As low as a snake's belly means _feeling very sad._

5. When I heard one of the hands had found Ted, I took off for the corral like a scalded cat! Now I could ride again! Like a scalded cat means _as fast as I could go._

Page 39

Off to the Races

Herbert was tired of always being the last one to get anywhere. He was tired of all his friends calling him Pokey. He was especially tired of Harriet making fun of the way he crawled along.

So Herbert decided to do something about it. He decided to practice running. He drew a line in the dirt with his front toes. He stood behind the line. He said to himself. "Ready. Set. Go!" Herbert practiced sprinting over the line and racing down the path. "It sure would be a lot easier if I didn't have to carry this old shell around on my back," Herbert muttered. But he didn't quit. He kept practicing.

So the next time, Herbert was ready when Harriet said, "Herbert, all you do is crawl along."

"I challenge you to a race," he said.

Harriet hopped up and down laughing. "It won't be a race," she said. "I know I'll win, paws down."

"We'll just see about that," said Herbert.

The next morning, with all their friends gathered for the race, Herbert and Harriet lined up side by side. Harriet was still laughing. Herbert clamped his jaws together and looked down the trail.

"Go!" the crowd shouted. Herbert pushed off with his four feet. He was off to a great start. Harriet fell behind. But that only lasted a moment. Soon Harriet bounced past Herbert.

"You are so pokey," she yelled back.

Herbert watched her race away and out of sight. At first he felt like hiding his head in his shell. But he kept going as fast as he could. After a few minutes, he spotted Harriet. She was sitting under a tree, nibbling a carrot.

As Herbert hurried by her, Harriet yelled, "You go ahead. I'll catch up after I finish my snack."

Herbert kept going. He could see the finish line. All their friends were waiting to see who would win. Herbert remembered all the things he'd practiced as he sprinted for the line. He knew Herbert was close behind. He lunged forward.

"Herbert is the winner!" yelled all his friends. "Hurray for Herbert!"

Page 40

Troubles

"Mom, may I go with Amy to the movie today?" Jill asked.

"Yes," said Mom.

"Oh, boy! Today is going to be a great day," Jill said. Her mom gave her money to buy popcorn. Jill put it in her coat pocket and ran all the way to Amy's house.

Amy's mother bought tickets for both girls. Amy and Jill went to buy popcorn, but when Jill reached into her pocket for her money it was gone. Instead, she found a hole in her pocket.

After the movie, the two girls walked to Amy's house. It was four o'clock when they got there. "I can stay until five o'clock," Jill told her friend. "Mom wants me home to help with supper."

The two girls decided to eat some cookies and play a game. Jill forgot to watch the time. When she heard the phone ring, she looked at the clock. "Oh, no!" she moaned. "I bet that's Mom." She jumped up and knocked the cookie plate off the table. The plate broke. Jill's mouth quivered as she looked at the mess. "I'm sorry," she whispered.

Answer each question with a complete sentence.

1. How did Jill feel at the beginning of the story? _Jill felt very excited._

2. What happened to Jill's popcorn money? _It fell out of the hole in her pocket._

3. Why did Jill think it was her mom on the phone? _She saw she was late already._

4. How did Jill feel when she broke the plate? _She felt sad._

5. Circle the answer that best tells how Jill probably felt about her day.
It was a bad day.   It was a boring day.   (It was a great day.)

Page 38

Off to the Races (cont.)

Draw a picture of Herbert.

Picture of a tortoise.

List 2 clues that told you about Herbert.
He is pokey.
He felt like hiding his head in his shell.

Draw a picture of Harriet.

Picture of a hare.

List 2 clues that told you about Harriet.
Harriet hops and bounces.
She eats carrots.

Complete the following.

1. What is another name for this story? _The Tortoise and the Hare._

2. How do you think Herbert felt when his friends called him Pokey? _He felt angry, hurt, sad._

3. Why did Herbert feel like hiding his head in his shell? _He was embarrassed/thought he would lose the race._

4. How did all of Herbert's friends feel when he won the race? _They were surprised and happy._

5. How do you think Harriet felt when Herbert won the race? _She was embarrassed & humiliated._

Page 41

48